NAVIGATING THE VOYAGE OF MUN

A YOUNG DELEGATE'S GUIDE TO MODEL UNITED NATIONS

ANAS DHORAJIWALA

ISBN 979-8-89133-610-0

CONTENTS

AUTHOR'S NOTE

Embarking on the MUNning Odyssey :)

In a time where the world evolves with every dawn, where threads of connectivity weave nations tighter, and where the echoes of decisions resonate globally, it's essential for budding leaders to decode the labyrinth of international ties. While classroom walls, weighty textbooks, and scholarly lectures provide windows into this universe, there exists a dynamic, immersive, and enlightening gateway that stands as a beacon for the youth: the Model United Nations, fondly christened as MUN.

MUN is not just a stage; it's a portal. It invites young adventurers to don the mantles of diplomats, immersing them in the tapestry of global conundrums. But, to truly dance in the MUN arena is not merely to debate. It's to master the elegant dance of 'MUNning'. Imagine MUN as a grand, sprawling galaxy. Here, 'MUNning' becomes your starship, guiding you through the nebulous challenges. It's not just a task; it's a journey of discovery. A trifecta of research, eloquence, and negotiation, it sharpens young intellects, molding them to reason with finesse, interact with grace, and sculpt pathways through global mazes.

As we embark on this exploration, let's illuminate the three guiding stars that every impactful orator and visionary leader cherishes:

1. **Empathy:** To not just hear, but to listen and feel the emotions and motivations of others.

2. **Knowledge:** A well-spring of facts, perspectives, and histories, equipping them to reason and respond.

3. **Adaptability:** The nimbleness to change course, to evolve strategies, and to find harmony even amidst discord.

Harnessing these will not only make you a luminary in the MUN cosmos but will also chart your trajectory in the vast universe of leadership.

Chapter 1

EMBARKING ON THE MUN VOYAGE FOR YOUNG EXPLORERS

A. Setting Sail with Knowledge:

Before any MUN adventurer can voice their thoughts, negotiate terms, or even form a plan, they must fill their treasure chest with knowledge. Like a sailor scanning the seas, mapping out routes, and understanding the tides, a brilliant MUN participant must know the history, discern the subtle dances of diplomacy, and keep an ear to the ground for the latest worldwide tales.

In the vast ocean of Model UN topics, it can seem like you're setting sail into an endless horizon. And while many charts *(research sources)* of this sea are designed for seasoned captains *(scholars and professionals)*, worry not! I have crafted a compass to guide young navigators like you. By understanding the five cardinal points of MUN research, you'll be well-equipped to represent your nation and draft legendary resolutions.

i. Crafting Your Nation's Storybook: Country Profile

Trusted Maps and Charts:

- CIA World Factbook
- JSTOR

Every nation has a tale to tell, and as its ambassador, you must narrate it with pride and accuracy. Drawing a detailed sketch of your nation ensures you grasp its heart and soul. Let's embark on this discovery:

Mapping the Terrain: Geographical Overview

4. What name does your nation proudly wear?
5. Which corner of our vast world does it call home?
6. How vast are its lands?
7. Which neighboring lands lie close to its borders?
8. Can you paint a picture of its landscapes and climates?

Steering the Ship: Political Landscape

1. When did the dawn of your nation rise?
2. Which form of rule steers its course?
3. Who are its guiding stars (notable leaders)?
4. How many guardians (military personnel) stand watch?
5. Which nations are friends in fair weather and foes in storms?
6. Where lies its heart (capital city)?

Song and Dance: Cultural Insights

1. How many souls call it home?
2. What myriad stories (ethnic groups) make up its tapestry?
3. In which tongue do its tales mostly echo?

4. Are there other dialects that color its stories?

5. Which grand cities bustle with life and tales?

The Treasure Trove: Economic Outlook

1. How sweet or harsh is life on its shores?

2. How rich are its coffers (GDP)?

3. What gems (natural resources) does the land hide?

4. In which coins (currency) do its markets trade?

5. What goods come and go from its ports (imports and exports)?

6. Which shores (trading partners) does it trade tales with most often?

By answering these riddles, young explorer, you will not only map out your nation's tale but will also be armed with stories, facts, and legends to share on your MUN voyage.

ii. Discovering Your Topic's Story

Every topic in the Model UN has its own fascinating tale, and it's your job to uncover it. This means diving deep into your topic, like a detective trying to solve a mystery. Here's how you can do it:

What's the Tale About? Begin by understanding what your topic is really about. If it were a book, what would be its title?

Topic's Key Clues:

Think of words or phrases that pop up frequently about your topic. For example, if your topic is 'global warming,' words like 'climate change,' 'greenhouse gases,' and 'carbon footprint' might be key clues. Also, ask fun questions like, "What's causing this big fuss?" or "Who and where are most affected by this?"

Trusty Detective Tools:

Now, remember to always use reliable tools for your detective work. Think of it like using a magnifying glass that shows things clearly. While Wikipedia, news, and blogs are like binoculars that give a broader view, always cross-check facts with more detailed sources!

iii. Time-Travelling to Past Actions

Let's imagine you have a time machine! Your next mission is to go back in time and see what the big superheroes (like the United Nations) have done about your topic before.

Looking Back:

Find out about previous heroic attempts like the UN resolutions or treaties the world agreed upon. Did they work? Why or why not?

Mission Tools: Some helpful tools on this journey are old UN resolutions, reports written by top leaders, and records of big meetings. And if you're curious to dig deeper, there's a cool article about using UN sources to discover more!

iv. Your Country's Super Stand

This part is like understanding a superhero's secret identity. What does your country really think about your topic?

Finding the Super Identity:

Dive into your country's secrets by checking what its leaders or representatives have said about your topic. Maybe there's a statement or a big speech that can be your guiding star.

More Detective Tools: The UN has some cool records of speeches and votes, so you can see if your country gave a thumbs-up or thumbs-down on certain decisions.

v. Crafting Super Solutions

Alright, young hero, here comes the most thrilling part! Now, you get to imagine solutions for the challenges your topic presents. This is where you wear your superhero cape and think of creative ways to save the day.

Dream Big, But Stay Grounded:

While dreaming of solutions, make sure they are practical. Maybe there's an old solution that needs a magic touch, or perhaps a new idea that could change everything!

Where to Find Ideas? Apart from the UN's actions, check out what non-profit groups (NGOs) are doing. They often have some super cool ideas. Think Tanks and university articles can also spark some inspiration.

IMPORTANT NOTE!

Remember, young delegate, every topic is like an adventure waiting to be explored. So, wear your detective hat, time-travelling goggles, superhero cape, and embark on this thrilling journey!

Your research across these five categories should all go in to your "Research Binder", which you should put together to prepare for a conference.

FUN ACTIVITY :)

Hey Adventurers!

Are you ready for a fun activity to end our chapter? Grab a sheet of paper and some colors, because we're about to create our very own **"MUN Adventure Map!"**

What's this adventure map, you ask?

Well, it's a special map that'll help us remember everything we've learned today. You know how explorers use maps to find treasures? Our treasures are the exciting things we've just discovered about MUN!

Let's get started!

1. **Draw Your Path:** Imagine a winding path on your paper. This is your MUN journey! Think of the path like a story - starting from knowing nothing about your country to becoming its superhero!

2. **Add Landmarks:** Remember the five big things we talked about today? Like your country's profile and the big challenges (topics) in the world? For each of these, draw a small symbol or picture.

   - For *Country Profile*, you might draw a flag.

   - For *Topic Discovery*, how about a light bulb, because it's an idea?

   - Past Actions: A clock or calendar page.

   - For *Country's Stand*, how about a speech bubble?

   - For Solutions, a star or toolbox.

3. **Connect the Dots:** Now, make a winding path that goes through each of your symbols. It's like connecting the dots, but with a twist!

4. **A Little Note:** Beside each symbol, write down one thing you remember about it. It could be a fun fact, or even something that surprised you!

Guess what? By the end of this, you'll have a cool map that tells the story of your MUN journey! And whenever you look at it, you'll remember our fun adventure today.

I can't wait to see your maps! Remember, there's no right or wrong here. It's all about having fun and exploring what you've learned. Happy drawing!

Chapter 2

HARMONIZING DISCOURSE AND DIPLOMACY: THE DUAL ARTS OF DEBATE AND NEGOTIATION IN MUN

A. The Arena of Discourse: Debating in MUN

In an ever-evolving world of ideas, where knowledge becomes the shining armor, the realm of debate emerges as the grand coliseum where intellects clash and thoughts spar. Within the halls of MUN, 'MUNning' beckons young delegates not merely to speak, but to illuminate, to challenge, and above all, to lend an ear. Amidst the symphony of diverse voices, the craft lies in resonating distinctively, all while embracing the melodies of others. This artistry, once mastered within MUN's walls, becomes a beacon guiding real-world champions.

i. The Symphony of Discourse

MUN debate is not just about the crescendo of a powerful argument; it's the harmonious ballet of ideas. Delegates are taught not just to project but to reflect, echoing the sentiments of nations they represent. It's in this dance of words that the true beauty of 'MUNning' unfurls.

Assertiveness:

At the very foundation of impactful discourse lies the ability to speak with a resolute voice that refuses to waver. Assertiveness is not just about volume but the resonance of conviction. It's about delivering statements that are robustly backed by knowledge and research. In the MUN arena, an assertive delegate ensures that their points stand tall, carrying the authority of both knowledge and belief, while steering clear of aggressive confrontations. The true essence of assertiveness is to let every word emanate the confidence of one's stance, painting a compelling picture that beckons others to take note.

Critical Engagement:

Engaging with an issue goes beyond mere surface-level understanding. Critical engagement demands an in-depth analysis, a knack for discerning nuances, and the agility to adapt one's arguments based on the flow of discourse. In the dynamic realm of MUN, where views are constantly shared and challenged, delegates must not just defend but also enrich their perspectives. This involves understanding the crux of opposing arguments, deconstructing them, and crafting even stronger counterpoints. It's a dance of the mind, where thoughts and ideas intertwine to create an enriched understanding of the topic at hand.

Active Listening:

In the symphony of voices that fill the MUN chamber, the art of active listening is often the unsung hero. It's not just about hearing words, but truly understanding the emotions, intentions, and concerns behind them. An effective delegate knows that every statement from another country or representative can be a window into their priorities and stances. By actively listening, one can discern the underlying tones, appreciate the essence of diverse viewpoints, and respond in a way that's both informed and empathetic. It's the silent bridge that connects differing shores, fostering understanding and collaboration in a world of diverse voices.

Mastery in this arena not only crowns you a champion of MUN deliberations but also readies you for the grander stages of global leadership.

ii. The Delicate Dance: Mastering Negotiation in MUN

Beneath the tapestry of international dynamics, it isn't merely about the might of a roaring voice, but the finesse of the compelling whisper. MUNning transcends the art of mere speaking, bringing to the forefront the subtle yet potent power of negotiation. The stage is set not for a clash but for a collaboration, where words weave webs of alliances, mutual understanding unfolds, and the timeless dance of give-and-take is choreographed with precision.

The Ballet of Diplomacy:

MUN's very heart pulsates with negotiation. It's a world where delegates aren't just speakers but diplomatic dancers, moving gracefully across the floor of mutual interests, extending hands for partnerships, and synchronizing steps for common goals.

Strategic Alliance-Building:

In the labyrinth of international diplomacy, connections are key. However, forging these connections requires more than just a handshake; it demands a strategic mind. Strategic alliance-building is the adept skill of discerning allies even before they voice their views, identifying the underlying currents that unite countries with shared interests or mutual benefits. This is where the MUN delegate, like a seasoned diplomat, crafts partnerships, drawing upon shared goals and intertwining strengths to bolster their collective voice. In a world where unity often carries more weight than isolated voices, the alliances forged can amplify a nation's stance and pave the way for joint triumphs.

Empathetic Understanding:

Beyond the boundaries and diverse cultures, at the core of every nation's stance in MUN lies a shared human experience. To truly excel in international diplomacy, a delegate must master the subtle art of empathetic understanding. It's about deeply resonating with the emotions, challenges, and histories of other nations. By stepping into another's shoes, delegates transcend mere transactional interactions, nurturing bonds founded on genuine appreciation and understanding. This not only aids in formulating more inclusive solutions but also nurtures trust – the cornerstone of enduring diplomatic relations.

Balanced Compromise:

Negotiation is an intricate dance, where assertiveness meets flexibility. In the world of MUN, as in the broader realm of international relations, hardline stances rarely yield fruitful results. The essence of balanced compromise lies in discerning that delicate equilibrium between maintaining one's core objectives and allowing room for adjustments. It's about recognizing that diplomacy thrives on give-and-take, where mutual respect and shared gains are prioritized over individual triumphs. The seasoned delegate knows that the most resilient resolutions are those woven from threads of mutual concessions, where every nation feels both heard and valued. It's in this balance that the true spirit of international collaboration flourishes.

When young MUNners fine-tune this intricate ballet, they aren't just prepping for the applause at the end of a conference. They're gearing up for the ovations that await them in the grand amphitheaters of tomorrow's global leadership.

FUN ACTIVITY :)

Hey Future Diplomats!

Ever thought of yourself as both a musician and a dancer on the world stage? Today, we're diving deep into the magical world of debate and negotiation in MUN! By the end of our chapter, you're going to be both a master of discourse and a delicate negotiator. But first, let's have a bit of fun with an activity I call **"Diplomatic Charades!"**

The Art of Diplomatic Charades

1. **Pick Your Role:** You can choose to be a speaker from a country or someone trying to negotiate a deal.

2. **Choose Your Topic:** Grab a bowl. Inside, ask your seniors to put in some slips with different topics (like "saving the environment" or "building a playground"). Pick one, but shh! Don't tell anyone what you've got!

3. **Time to Act!**

    - **For Debaters:** Without speaking, try to act out and express your feelings about the topic using only your body. Can you show excitement, concern, or determination without saying a word?

    - **For Negotiators:** Imagine you're trying to convince someone to help you. How would you approach them? With a handshake? A smile? A compelling gesture? Show us!

4. **Let's Guess:** Everyone else will try to guess what you're trying to convey. Are you happy with the playground idea or concerned about the environment?

5. **Discuss and Reflect:** After each turn, chat about what you saw. What made a big impression? What gestures or actions caught your attention?

Why are we doing this?

This activity helps us understand that, just like in MUN, sometimes it's not only about the words we say but also about how we say them. Body language, gestures, and even a simple nod can tell a whole story!

Remember, young diplomats, in the world of MUN, and in life, understanding and collaborating with others is a beautiful dance, and everyone has their unique rhythm. Now, let's continue our journey to becoming the future stars of global leadership!

Chapter 3

THE BIRTH AND GROWTH OF THE UNITED NATIONS

Introduction

The United Nations (UN) stands tall as a symbol of international cooperation and hope for a better world. But how did this global organization come to be? This chapter traces the history of the UN, helping you understand its origins and the events that shaped it.

The League of Nations: A Throwback to When Nations First Tried to Unite

Genesis of the League of Nations: When the World Wanted Peace

Picture this: World War I, the "Great War," had just ended. The world, scarred and weary from years of conflict, was desperate for peace. Out of this collective hope, the League of Nations was born - birthed within the Treaty of Versailles. Think of it as the world's first official attempt at creating a 'global team' dedicated to peace.

What the League Stood For

Imagine a group of nations making a pact that if one got into trouble, the others would swoop in to help. That was the core idea behind the League's Covenant. This wasn't just about playing defense against aggression; it was also about building a better world. They were all about promoting health, better working conditions, and sparking brilliant international projects.

The League's Blueprint

So, how did the League function? It was a bit like high school:

1. **The Assembly:** The school assembly where every nation had a say. They brainstormed policies and even decided how to spend their money.

2. **The Council:** The student council – handling disputes, ensuring no one was bullied, and making those big, critical decisions.

3. **The Secretariat:** The administration – managing day-to-day stuff. And yes, there were clubs! Think of agencies like the International Labour Organization as the 'eco-club,' working towards specific global goals.

The Bright Side: Wins of the League

Before we delve into its challenges, let's give some credit where it's due! The League prevented a conflict over the Aaland Islands, hosted a global disarmament event (even if it didn't go as planned), and stepped up humanitarian game by helping refugees, fighting diseases, and controlling drugs. They were the OGs in some critical areas of international relations!

The Flip Side: Hurdles and Stumbles

But, like every story, there were villains and obstacles. One of the biggest twists? The U.S., even with President Wilson being one of the masterminds behind the League, didn't join because of some home drama. Also, their rulebook had some serious flaws. Imagine trying to make a decision in a group chat where EVERYONE has to agree – yep, that was the League. Plus, they didn't have a 'security squad' or an army. Their idea of punishing rule-breakers through economic sanctions? Not always effective. And then, the big bad wolves: the rise of dictatorships in Germany, Italy, and Japan. The League struggled, and it showed.

The Final Countdown and a New Dawn

By the time the late 1930s rolled around, it was clear the League's influence was, let's just say, not on fleek. As Europe's political atmosphere got tenser, the League struggled to keep the peace. When World War II erupted in 1939, it was like the final season of a TV show where the original mission of the protagonist, in this case, the League, got lost in the chaos. This world catastrophe pretty much marked its exit.

But here's the plot twist: The League's legacy wasn't just about its shortcomings. From its ashes rose the phoenix that is the United Nations, a refined vision of global collaboration and unity. The League's journey, with all its highs and lows, gave the world invaluable lessons and set the stage for today's international system.

So, next time you think about global unity, remember the League - the first ever team that dared to dream big for the world.

Founding the United Nations: A New Hope for Global Peace

In the bleak aftermath of World War II, with the horrors of global conflict still fresh in memory, the world yearned for a lasting mechanism to ensure peace and prevent future wars. This collective desire led to the conception of an international organization dedicated to fostering global cooperation: The United Nations.

San Francisco Summit: A Global Gathering

In the spring of 1945, San Francisco became the focal point of global attention. The city, known for its iconic Golden Gate Bridge, hosted a conference of paramount importance - the United Nations Conference on International Organization. Imagine the scene: Delegates from 50 countries, each carrying the hopes and aspirations of their people, converging in packed conference rooms, fervently debating clauses and terms. These weren't just discussions; they were the initial steps toward a new world order.

Drafting the Charter: Crafting the Vision

This wasn't a typical conference. The representatives gathered in San Francisco had a monumental task at hand: drafting the United Nations Charter - the foundational treaty of the UN. The Charter was more than just a document; it was a manifestation of global unity, an articulation of shared values and principles. It encapsulated the world's commitment to maintaining peace, upholding human rights, and fostering social and economic development. The delegates spent weeks deliberating, negotiating, and fine-tuning every word, ensuring that it reflected the collective will for a peaceful future.

The Birth of the United Nations: A Symbolic Moment

On June 26, 1945, a historic moment unfolded. The drafted Charter was ready for endorsement. In a solemn ceremony, representatives of the 50 nations affixed their signatures, marking the birth of the United Nations. But the story didn't end there. For the UN to officially come into existence, the Charter had to be ratified by the majority of the signatory countries, including the five permanent members of the Security Council. By October 24, 1945, this criterion was met, and the United Nations officially sprung to life, heralding a new era of international collaboration.

United Nations Day: Celebrating Unity

October 24th isn't just another date on the calendar. It's a day of global celebration, commemorating the birth of the UN and the ideals it represents. Every year, as United Nations Day rolls around, it serves as a poignant reminder of our shared commitment to peace, equality, and sustainable development. It's a day to reflect on our collective achievements and recommit to the lofty goals that the United Nations embodies.

In a world marred by conflicts and divisions, the foundation of the United Nations was a beacon of hope, signaling the possibility of a united, collaborative future. Today, as we navigate complex global challenges, the spirit and vision behind the UN's inception remain as relevant and vital as ever.

The UN is like a big team where countries come together to solve problems and make the world a better place. It's a symbol of hope and cooperation, showing us that when we work together, we can achieve great things.

Remember, the UN is not just about meetings and decisions; it's about creating a future where everyone, including you, can live in peace and prosperity.

FUN ACTIVITY :)

United Nations Passport to Peace!

Objective:

We're going on an imaginary journey around the world with the United Nations! As we explore this chapter's story, create your very own UN Passport. At each checkpoint, you'll discover a fun fact or do a mini-activity. Let's start our adventure!

Materials:

- A small booklet or a few sheets of paper stapled together to make your "passport."

- Colors: crayons, colored pencils, and markers.

- Stickers or stamps (optional).

- A pen or pencil for writing.

Procedure:

1. **Craft Your Passport:**

    - Design the front cover with "UN Passport to Peace" and your name.

    - On the first page, draw a little picture of yourself as the "Passport Holder."

    - Number each page – these are your checkpoints!

2. **First Checkpoint: The League of Nations:**

    - Draw a big globe. Around it, sketch or stick flags of a few countries. Write, "The first team for peace!"

    - Fun Fact: The League of Nations was created after World War I as the world's first attempt to maintain peace.

3. **Second Checkpoint: San Francisco Summit:**

    - Draw a picture of the Golden Gate Bridge.

    - Fun Activity: Pretend you're a delegate from your favorite country. Write down one rule you want everyone to follow for global peace.

4. **Third Checkpoint: Drafting the UN Charter:**

    - Sketch a big book and label it "UN Charter."

    - Fun Fact: The Charter is like the rulebook for the United Nations, telling countries how to work together for peace and progress.

5. **Fourth Checkpoint: Birth of the United Nations:**

    - Draw a big birthday cake with "UN" written on it.

    - Fun Activity: Sing a birthday song to the United Nations. You can even make one up!

6. **Fifth Checkpoint: United Nations Day:**

    - Sketch a calendar, marking October 24th with a star or sticker.

    - Fun Fact: Every year, October 24th celebrates the day when the UN officially began its mission of bringing nations together.

Final Step: Passport Stamps:

As you finish each checkpoint, give yourself a stamp or sticker on that page. Once you've completed all checkpoints, you're now a mini UN explorer!

Closing:

Remember, just like you now have a passport full of adventures and discoveries, the United Nations has been on a long journey to help the world be a better place. Each checkpoint you've marked is a reminder of the steps they took, and guess what? You're now a part of this big story too!

Chapter 4

THE CORNERSTONES OF THE UNITED NATIONS

The establishment of the United Nations (UN) was not just about creating another international organization. Instead, it was a profound commitment by nations worldwide to ensure that the horrors of two World Wars would never be repeated. To comprehend the UN's significance, we must delve into its primary objectives and the organs it instituted to achieve them.

The Visionary Compass of the United Nations

The inception of the United Nations (UN) in the mid-20th century marked a transformative moment in global diplomacy. Born from the ashes of two cataclysmic world wars, the UN emerged as a beacon of hope, illuminating a pathway to a more harmonious and interconnected world. To truly understand the importance and the mission of the UN, one must dive deep into the foundational objectives that underpin its existence. These objectives are not mere aspirational statements; they serve as the compass guiding the UN in its global endeavors.

Maintaining International Peace and Security:

A scarred world, having witnessed the devastations of two wars, demanded nothing more than peace. At the core of the UN's mission is an unwavering commitment to preventing conflicts that can escalate into large-scale wars. But the UN's vision goes beyond just conflict prevention; it emphasizes the importance of disarmament. By advocating for the reduction and eventual elimination of weapons of mass destruction, the UN aims to tackle the very root of warfare, minimizing the potential for future violent confrontations.

Developing Friendly Relations among Nations:

In a diverse world filled with nations of different cultures, histories, and aspirations, the potential for misunderstandings is rife. Recognizing this, the UN aspired to be the bridge that connects nations. By promoting mutual respect, understanding, and cooperation, the UN fosters an environment where nations can celebrate their differences and find common ground, creating a global tapestry woven with threads of diplomacy and friendship.

Achieving International Cooperation:

The challenges of the modern world, such as economic disparities, health crises, and cultural rifts, recognize no borders. They are global issues requiring global solutions. The UN's vision in this realm is broad yet focused – to bring nations together, pooling resources, knowledge, and expertise, to address and solve these multifaceted challenges. Whether it's combating a pandemic, fighting against poverty, or preserving the world's cultural heritage, the UN serves as the rallying point, uniting the world in collective action.

Being a Center for Harmonizing Actions:

In an orchestra, each instrument plays its part, yet all come together to create a symphony. Similarly, with the world's nations each having their unique policies, goals, and agendas, there's a need for a conductor to ensure harmony. The UN fulfills this role by streamlining global efforts, ensuring that individual actions of nations align with shared global goals. It's here that policies are coordinated, best practices are shared, and collaborative efforts are maximized to achieve the best outcomes for the planet and its inhabitants.

The United Nations is not merely a byproduct of history; it's a visionary institution designed with the future in mind. Its foundational objectives reflect humanity's shared dreams and aspirations for a peaceful, cooperative, and prosperous world. Each objective, while distinct, intertwines with the others, painting a holistic picture of the world the UN seeks to create. As we navigate the complexities of the 21st century, the UN's compass – its guiding objectives – will remain crucial in steering humanity towards a brighter, shared future.

The Architectural Pillars: Major Organs of the United Nations

In the vast edifice of international diplomacy and cooperation that is the United Nations (UN), certain structural pillars hold the weight and ensure its stability. These foundational structures, the principal organs of the UN, each play a distinct role in the organization's broader mission. Their formation was not merely an administrative necessity but a reflection of the diverse functions the UN was envisioned to perform in global affairs. Let's delve into the intricacies of these organs, which together form the cohesive backbone of the UN.

1. **General Assembly** - The Grand Concourse of Nations: Think of the General Assembly as the world's most inclusive forum, a platform where all member states, irrespective of their size or

influence, have an equal voice. Every year, leaders from around the globe converge in this arena to discuss pressing global issues, from climate change to peacekeeping. Resolutions passed here, though often not legally binding, carry the weight of international opinion and set the tone for global norms.

2. **Security Council** - The Guardians of Peace: Arguably one of the most potent arms of the UN, the Security Council bears the heavy responsibility of maintaining international peace and security. Comprising five permanent members (the P5 – China, France, Russia, the UK, and the US) and ten elected members, the Council has the unique power to authorize military interventions and impose sanctions. The requirement for its permanent members to agree on substantive matters ensures that major powers are in concert, but it also sometimes leads to criticism due to potential deadlocks.

3. **International Court of Justice (ICJ)** - The Beacon of Global Justice: Located in the tranquil surroundings of The Hague, Netherlands, the ICJ is the UN's principal judicial organ. It isn't a criminal court but one that settles legal disputes between states. Its rulings, grounded in international law, help clarify ambiguities, uphold treaties, and guide state behavior. Additionally, the ICJ offers advisory opinions on legal questions referred by authorized UN organs and specialized agencies.

4. **Secretariat** - The Operational Engine: Behind the scenes of the vast machinery of the UN, the Secretariat ensures the smooth functioning of all its programs and initiatives. Headed by the Secretary-General, arguably the world's top diplomat, this organ manages the day-to-day affairs of the UN. From peacekeeping operations to humanitarian relief, the Secretariat's dedicated staff work tirelessly to implement the mandates of the other organs.

5. **Economic and Social Council (ECOSOC)** - The Conduit for Global Progress: As its name suggests, ECOSOC focuses on the world's economic, social, and environmental issues. It serves as a

platform for fostering international cooperation in developmental areas, ensuring that all nations move forward together. Through its specialized agencies, like the World Health Organization (WHO) and the United Nations Educational, Scientific, and Cultural Organization (UNESCO), ECOSOC addresses diverse challenges like health crises, educational needs, and cultural preservation.

6. **Trusteeship Council** - The Guardian of Transition: Though it has suspended its operations since the last of the 11 trust territories attained self-government in 1994, the Trusteeship Council played a pivotal role in overseeing territories that were not self-governing post World War II. It ensured that the inhabitants of these territories were provided with adequate conditions for self-governance, helping many regions transition smoothly to independence.

The major organs of the UN, in their distinctive capacities, together compose the symphony of global cooperation. Each organ, with its unique mandate, is a testament to the UN's comprehensive approach to global challenges. As the world evolves, facing both age-old and emerging challenges, these architectural pillars of the United Nations continue to uphold its lofty ideals, steering the world toward peace, justice, and shared prosperity.

FUN ACTIVITY :)

Objective:

To help you understand the core objectives and main organs of the United Nations by creating their own UN Clubhouse

Materials Needed:

- Large cardboard boxes or sheets
- Crayons, markers, and paints
- Printed logos or symbols of each UN organ
- Sticky notes or small cards
- Decorative items (glitter, stickers, ribbons, etc.)
- A world map (can be printed or drawn)

Instructions:

1. **Build the Clubhouse:**
   - Use cardboard boxes or sheets to create the structure of your clubhouse. This can be as simple as a single box or a series of boxes connected together.

2. **Decorating the Clubhouse:**
   - Paint or color the outside of the boxes in the UN's signature blue.
   - Stick the world map on one side of the clubhouse.

3. **Organ Cards Creation:**
   - On sticky notes or small cards, write down the names of each of the major UN organs.
   - Draw or stick the printed logos or symbols next to each name.
   - On the back, write a fun fact or simple sentence about what that organ does. For instance, "The General Assembly is like the biggest classroom where every country has a seat!"

4. **Treasure Hunt:**

    - Hide the organ cards around your house or garden.

    - Let your friends or family members find these cards. When they find a card, they should read the fact aloud and then stick it onto the world map in your clubhouse.

5. **Role-playing:**

    - Once all the cards are found and stuck onto the map, gather in the clubhouse.

    - Pretend to be leaders of different countries. Talk about how you would work together to make the world a better place. Use the UN organs as your guide. For instance, someone can pretend to be a part of the "Security Council" and talk about keeping peace.

6. **Snack Time:**

    - Every meeting needs snacks! Take a break and enjoy some treats together. Maybe even try snacks from different countries to celebrate the international spirit of the UN.

Conclusion:

End your UN clubhouse day by discussing what you all learned. Talk about the importance of working together and understanding people from different parts of the world. Remember, even as kids, everyone can make a difference!

Note:

Parents or older siblings can help younger kids with setting up and understanding some of the more complex concepts. The goal is to make it fun, engaging, and informative at a level that's suitable for the child's age and understanding.

Chapter 5

TRIUMPHS OF TOGETHERNESS: MAJOR ACHIEVEMENTS OF THE UNITED NATIONS

In the sprawling annals of international cooperation, the United Nations stands out as an emblematic entity, striving to shape a world marked by peace, solidarity, and progress. Over the decades, the UN has been at the forefront of myriad global challenges, mediating in conflicts, pioneering social reforms, and amplifying the voices of the marginalized. As students of history, politics, or international relations, one can glean a wealth of knowledge and insights by studying the UN's vast repository of resolutions, which not only reflect its achievements but also chronicle the evolving dynamics of global politics.

1. Peacekeeping Missions: Guardians in the Battle Zones

The United Nations, throughout its existence, has donned multiple hats, but one of its most distinctive and impactful roles has been in the realm of peacekeeping. Venturing into some of the most volatile terrains, the UN Peacekeeping Forces have consistently epitomized international collaboration in the service of peace. By dissecting some of the significant peacekeeping missions – Cambodia, Liberia, and the former Yugoslavia – we can truly fathom the breadth and depth of the UN's efforts.

Cambodia: From Turmoil to Tranquility

In the early 1990s, Cambodia was emerging from decades of conflict, including the harrowing reign of the Khmer Rouge, which left nearly two million dead. The UN Transitional Authority in Cambodia (UNTAC) was established in 1992 to ensure the implementation of a comprehensive political settlement, facilitate the repatriation of refugees, and organize free and fair elections. With a multi-dimensional approach that encompassed civil administration, military, police, and human rights components, UNTAC played a pivotal role in transitioning Cambodia towards stability.

Liberia: Navigating a Path out of Civil War

Liberia, a nation scarred by two brutal civil wars resulting in the death and displacement of countless citizens, beckoned the UN's intervention in 2003. The UN Mission in Liberia (UNMIL) was mandated to support the implementation of the ceasefire agreement and the peace process. Beyond the standard peacekeeping duties, UNMIL was deeply involved in reforming the justice and security sectors, ensuring human rights, and facilitating humanitarian relief. Over its 15-year presence, Liberia transformed from a war-torn nation to one that conducted peaceful democratic transitions.

Former Yugoslavia: A Tangled Web of Ethnic Conflicts

The Balkans in the 1990s was a cauldron of ethnic tensions, leading to a series of conflicts that bewildered the international community. The dissolution of the Socialist Federal Republic of Yugoslavia resulted in bitter wars, marked by grave human rights abuses. In response, the UN instituted several missions, notably the United Nations Protection Force (UNPROFOR). This mission, one of the most challenging endeavors, was initially mandated to create conditions of peace and security favorable for the negotiation of an overall settlement. While the peacekeeping efforts faced numerous challenges, they highlighted the complexities of modern conflicts and set the stage for later, more comprehensive interventions like the NATO-led forces and the International Criminal Tribunal for the former Yugoslavia (ICTY), which aimed at prosecuting severe war crimes.

UN Peacekeeping missions have often been fraught with challenges. They tread the thin line between neutrality and intervention, sovereignty, and responsibility. However, the consistent thread running through all these missions is the unwavering commitment to prevent further bloodshed and provide war-ravaged nations a shot at peace and prosperity.

For students and scholars, these missions offer a kaleidoscopic view of international relations in action. They reveal the intricate dance of diplomacy, the formidable challenges of on-ground implementation, and the undying spirit of internationalism.

2. Eradication of Diseases: The War Against Epidemics

Battles aren't just fought on the frontlines with guns and tanks; some of the most consequential wars have been waged in the realm of public health. Spearheading these efforts has been the UN, primarily through the World Health Organization (WHO). The organization's determined forays into disease eradication offer glimpses of what can be achieved when nations unite for a common cause.

The Victory Over Smallpox

Smallpox, a deadly disease that left survivors with disfiguring scars, had haunted humanity for centuries. Its impact was such that it not only claimed lives but also shaped histories, cultures, and economies.

The global campaign against smallpox, initiated by the WHO in 1967, was an audacious endeavor. It required nations to pool resources, share data transparently, and frequently cross political and ideological divides.

The campaign was a blend of massive vaccination drives, rigorous surveillance, and innovative strategies tailored for local conditions. Within just over a decade, a disease that had once killed, blinded, and scarred millions was declared eradicated in 1980. This monumental achievement was not just a medical triumph but also showcased the might of international cooperation.

Polio: The Continuing Battle

Polio, another debilitating disease, primarily affects children, often resulting in permanent paralysis. The Global Polio Eradication Programme, launched in 1988, set forth on a mission to rid the world of this malady. With the collaborative efforts of national governments, the WHO, Rotary International, the CDC, and UNICEF, among others, the program has achieved remarkable successes.

From hundreds of thousands of reported cases in the 1980s, the numbers dwindled to just a few hundred by the 2010s. Several regions, once grappling with widespread polio cases, have been declared polio-free. The challenges in completely eradicating the disease remain, with pockets of resistance and hard-to-reach areas. Yet, the journey so far underscores the potential of global initiatives, innovation in vaccine delivery, and relentless grassroots campaigns.

A Multi-Pronged Approach to Public Health

Beyond these high-profile campaigns, the UN, through the WHO, has initiated a plethora of programs targeting a myriad of health concerns. From combating the spread of Ebola, instituting measures against the spread of HIV/AIDS, to the recent global mobilization against the COVID-19 pandemic – the organization has been at the forefront. These efforts encompass not just disease control but also health education, infrastructure development, and capacity building in countries with fragile healthcare systems.

For students and young professionals keen on public health, international relations, or medical research, there's a goldmine of information in the annals of the UN's health campaigns. Examining past resolutions, mission directives, and post-campaign evaluations can provide profound insights into the intricacies of global health initiatives. Such research doesn't just elucidate the medical aspects but also shines a light on the sociology of health, the economics of healthcare interventions, and the politics of international health diplomacy. It offers a holistic perspective on how global health challenges are approached, managed, and often overcome. In summation, the battles against diseases, while often less heralded than military or political feats, are equally significant in shaping our world. They remind us of our shared vulnerabilities as humans but, more importantly, of our indomitable spirit when united against common foes.

3. Human Rights Advocacy: The Voice for the Voiceless

The landscape of human rights has been fraught with challenges, yet it is here that the United Nations has emerged as a beacon of hope and an unwavering advocate for those silenced by oppression, discrimination, and violence. The journey, initiated with the Universal Declaration of Human Rights in 1948, has since encompassed myriad facets of human dignity, freedom, and equality.

The Universal Declaration of Human Rights (UDHR): A New Dawn

In the aftermath of World War II, a conflict that witnessed unparalleled atrocities, there was a collective yearning for a document that would champion the innate rights of every individual. The UDHR, adopted in 1948, was groundbreaking. For the first time in history, a document articulated the fundamental human rights that should be protected for all people, transcending boundaries, cultures, and ideologies. It set the tone for subsequent treaties, serving as both an aspirational vision and a foundational framework.

Treaties and Conventions: Setting the Standards

Over the decades, the broad principles of the UDHR were honed into specific treaties and conventions, each targeting distinct areas of human rights:

- **International Covenant on Civil and Political Rights (ICCPR) and International Covenant on Economic, Social and Cultural Rights (ICESCR):** Together with the UDHR, these form the International Bill of Human Rights, expanding on rights related to employment, family, culture, and freedom from torture, among others.

- **Convention on the Elimination of All Forms of Discrimination Against Women (CEDAW):** Often dubbed as the international bill of rights for women, CEDAW is a powerful tool against gender-based discrimination, advocating for women's rights in all spheres - political, economic, social, and cultural.

- **Convention on the Rights of the Child (CRC):** A testament to the UN's commitment to the youngest members of society, the CRC establishes rights related to health, education, and protection from abuse and exploitation.

- **Convention Relating to the Status of Refugees:** In a world increasingly marred by conflicts and displacement, this convention provides a protective framework for millions who have been forced to flee their homes, setting out their rights and the legal obligations of states.

- **Convention Against Torture and Other Cruel, Inhuman or Degrading Treatment or Punishment (CAT):** An unequivocal stand against one of the most heinous violations of human rights, this convention seeks to prevent and punish acts of torture.

Human Rights Council & Special Rapporteurs: Operationalizing Advocacy

The Human Rights Council, an inter-governmental body within the UN, is tasked with addressing human rights violations. Its Universal Periodic Review scrutinizes the human rights record of every UN member state, fostering a culture of accountability. Complementing this are the Special Rapporteurs - independent experts appointed to monitor and report on specific human rights themes or country situations. Their reports, often painstakingly detailed, shed light on overlooked issues, galvanizing international attention and action.

Students, researchers, and budding activists will find a treasure trove of resources in the UN's archives. Delving into past resolutions, debates, and reports provides a nuanced understanding of the evolution of human rights discourse. Such exploration reveals not just the victories, but also the challenges, compromises, and the ongoing struggles in the quest for universal human rights. The UN's endeavors in human rights advocacy underscore a profound truth: Rights are not mere abstract ideals but are vital for the fulfillment of human potential. In amplifying the voices of the marginalized and challenging structures of power, the UN continues to strive for a world where every individual's rights are realized and respected.

4. Sustainable Development Goals (SDGs): A Blueprint for a Better Future

In the kaleidoscope of challenges and endeavors that the world grapples with, the Sustainable Development Goals (SDGs) shine as a comprehensive tapestry of ambition, responsibility, and foresight. Adopted in 2015 as part of the 2030 Agenda for Sustainable Development, the 17 SDGs, backed by 169 specific targets, aim to weave together the diverse threads of the world's most pressing challenges and paint a future where prosperity and peace are shared by all.

Origins of the SDGs: Beyond the Millennium Development Goals (MDGs)

The roots of the SDGs lie in their predecessors, the Millennium Development Goals (MDGs). Adopted in 2000, the MDGs were an initial set of 8 goals targeting core areas of development, from eradicating extreme poverty and hunger to ensuring environmental sustainability. While they set the wheels of global cooperation in motion, their journey highlighted gaps and areas needing a more expansive and inclusive approach. Hence, the SDGs were conceived to be broader, deeper, and more holistic.

Navigating the 17 Goals: Unity in Diversity

The vast scope of the SDGs captures almost every facet of human and planetary well-being:

1. **No Poverty and Zero Hunger:** The foundational goals address the primary needs of human survival and dignity, striving to ensure that every individual has access to basic necessities and means for a decent life.

2. **Health, Education, and Gender Equality:** Recognizing the innate potential of every individual, these goals seek to nurture minds, bodies, and aspirations, while breaking the shackles of discrimination and disparities.

3. **Clean Water & Sanitation to Affordable & Clean Energy:** They are crucial for both human societies and the ecosystems they inhabit. Their availability ensures sustainable living and progress.

4. **Economic Goals like Decent Work & Economic Growth, and Industry, Innovation & Infrastructure:** These goals acknowledge that for societies to thrive, economic systems need to be equitable, robust, and forward-looking.

5. **Environmental Goals:** With Life Below Water, Life on Land, and Climate Action, the SDGs raise the clarion call for urgent action

to protect our planet, ensuring that the harmony of ecosystems is maintained for future generations.

6. **Peace, Justice & Strong Institutions:** Recognizing that development is sustainable only in an environment of peace and rule of law, this goal emphasizes the need for robust institutions that are transparent, accountable, and just.

Inclusivity and Interconnectedness: Leaving No One Behind

A distinctive feature of the SDGs is their emphasis on universality. Unlike the MDGs, which were primarily aimed at challenges in developing countries, the SDGs are global in nature, acknowledging that even advanced economies have areas for sustainable improvement. The principle of "Leaving No One Behind" underscores the commitment to reach the most vulnerable and marginalized first.

For students and researchers interested in understanding the nuances of global development, the UN's vast repositories on the SDGs are invaluable. Exploring old resolutions, tracking progress reports, and analyzing discussions can provide deep insights into the dynamics of global cooperation, the challenges of implementation, and the innovations driving change. The SDGs are not just a list of goals but a reflection of humanity's shared dreams. They challenge the world to think beyond borders, to imagine a future where prosperity is not at the expense of the planet, and where every individual, no matter their circumstances, can aspire for and achieve a life of dignity and purpose. Through the SDGs, the UN extends an invitation to all – governments, businesses, civil society, and individuals – to come together and shape a future that resonates with the best of human values and aspirations.

Delving Deeper: Resolutions as Keys to Global Diplomacy

For aspiring delegates participating in Model United Nations (MUN) and students of international relations, the UN's rich archive of resolutions is akin to an invaluable trove of diplomatic wisdom. Each resolution, passed after intense deliberations and negotiations, is a snapshot of the world's pulse at a specific juncture in history. These documents, crafted with precision and careful word choice, offer unique insights into the dynamics of international diplomacy and the myriad forces that shape global decisions.

Why Resolutions Matter: Beyond the Surface

While casual observers may see resolutions as mere formalities or statements of intent, seasoned MUNners and scholars recognize their deeper significance:

1. **Reflecting Global Sentiments:** Resolutions, especially those passed with overwhelming majorities, encapsulate the global consensus on pressing issues. They highlight the shared values, concerns, and aspirations of nations, transcending borders and politics.

2. **Documenting Geopolitical Evolution:** Examining resolutions chronologically offers a roadmap of shifting alliances, emerging powers, and evolving priorities. For instance, resolutions from the Cold War era showcase a distinct East-West divide, while more recent ones might highlight concerns about climate change or cybersecurity.

3. **Masterclass in Diplomatic Language:** The carefully chosen words in resolutions are the results of meticulous negotiation. They showcase the art of conveying firm stances without alienating member states, a skill vital for MUN participants and future diplomats.

A Gateway to Profound Insights

Diving into specific resolutions can be enlightening:

- Resolutions on the Korean War reveal the complexities of proxy conflicts during the Cold War era.

- Those concerning the Israel-Palestine conflict document decades of attempts to find a lasting peace in one of the world's most contentious regions.

- The deliberations surrounding the Rwandan genocide expose both the international community's failures and its subsequent resolve to prevent such atrocities.

A Beacon for Aspiring Diplomats

For MUN delegates, understanding past resolutions is crucial. It equips them to draft realistic and impactful resolutions in their committees. By tracing the evolution of language, understanding the positions of key players, and discerning the underlying diplomatic strategies, they can emulate the nuances of real-world diplomacy in their simulations.

Furthermore, analyzing resolutions helps MUN participants anticipate objections, craft persuasive arguments, and build coalitions, enhancing their overall MUN performance.

The United Nations, despite its imperfections, stands as a beacon of humanity's shared aspirations for a better world. Its resolutions, rich in history and insight, serve as invaluable tools for those keen on deciphering the intricate dance of diplomacy. For MUN participants and students alike, diving deep into these documents isn't just a research task; it's an expedition into the heart of global collaboration, offering lessons that are timeless and transformative.

FUN ACTIVITY :)

"Speech Puzzle Pieces"

Objective:

To prepare a speech by breaking it down into manageable "puzzle pieces," helping participants better organize their thoughts and improve their delivery.

Materials Needed:

- Index cards or sturdy paper cut into sizable squares (about the size of a coaster).

- Markers or pens.

- A timer (optional).

- A whiteboard or large paper pad (optional for group activities).

- Sticky tack or tape.

Instructions:

1. **Brainstorming Topics:**
   - Think of a topic you'd like to give a speech on. It could be anything from "The Importance of Recycling" to "My Favorite Memory." Write this at the top of your whiteboard or paper pad.

2. **Breaking Down the Topic:**
   - Consider the main points you want to cover in your speech. Each main point will become a "puzzle piece."
   - Write each point on a separate index card. Use one to three words, e.g., "Environmental Impact" for a speech on recycling.

3. **Elaborate Each Point:**
   - Take each card and spend 3-5 minutes (use the timer) jotting down sub-points or ideas related to that main point.

For example, under "Environmental Impact," you might list "wildlife preservation," "landfill issues," and "ocean pollution."

4. **Arrange the Puzzle:**

   - Place your cards on a table or floor and try different sequences to see which order makes the most sense for your speech. This physical act helps you visualize the flow of your speech and see where transitions are necessary.

5. **Connect the Dots:**

   - Think of transitions between each point. Write these transitions on separate cards. Place them between your main points. For instance, transitioning from "Environmental Impact" to "Recycling Methods," you might write, "Now that we understand the impact, let's explore how we can make a change."

6. **Opening and Conclusion:**

   - Your opening should hook your audience and introduce your topic. Create a card labeled "Introduction" and detail your opening statement.

   - Your conclusion should wrap up your main points and leave your audience with a final thought. Create another card labeled "Conclusion" and outline your closing remarks.

7. **Practice with the Puzzle:**

   - Using the sequence of cards, practice delivering your speech. As you go through each "puzzle piece," place the card on a wall or board using sticky tack or tape. This helps reinforce the sequence in your mind.

8. **Group Variation (optional):**

   - If done in a group setting, participants can exchange their "puzzle pieces" with peers. The challenge is to try to deliver someone else's speech using their organized cards. This adds an element of improvisation and tests how well each "puzzle" is organized.

The "Speech Puzzle Pieces" activity breaks down the often daunting task of preparing a speech into smaller, more manageable segments. By organizing thoughts physically and visually, it becomes easier to see the overall flow and structure of the speech, making the actual writing and delivering process more systematic and coherent.

Chapter 6

NAVIGATING THE MUN LANDSCAPE: CHOOSING THE RIGHT COMMITTEE

As you embark on the enriching journey of participating in a Model United Nations (MUN) conference, one of the pivotal decisions you'll need to make is selecting a committee. Your choice can profoundly influence your MUN experience, impacting everything from the topics you'll debate to the dynamics of the interactions you'll have. This chapter will guide you through the considerations and strategies to make an informed choice.

1. Understanding MUN Committees: A Brief Overview

Before diving into the selection process, it's essential to understand the diverse range of committees that MUN conferences usually offer:

- **General Assembly Committees (GA):** These are large, encompassing a vast number of delegates. GAs often discuss a wide range of global issues, from disarmament to economic and financial matters.

- **Specialized Committees:** These can range from the World Health Organization (WHO) to the International Monetary Fund (IMF). They tend to focus on specific thematic areas.

- **Crisis Committees:** Highly dynamic and fast-paced, these simulate real-time crises where delegates must respond promptly to evolving situations.

- **Historical Committees:** These recreate events from the past, asking delegates to debate issues with the knowledge and perspectives of that time.

2. Assessing Your Experience and Comfort Level

Your MUN experience can guide your committee choice:

- **Beginners:** If you're new to MUN, starting with a General Assembly might be beneficial. The broad topics and larger group dynamics can provide a solid introduction to MUN procedures.

- **Intermediate:** With some MUNs under your belt, you might explore specialized committees or smaller GAs to dive deeper into specific issues.

- **Advanced:** Experienced MUNners might relish the challenge of crisis committees or relive historical decisions in historical committees.

3. Passion and Interest

Choose a committee that sparks your curiosity or aligns with your passions. Whether you're deeply concerned about global health issues or passionate about economic policies, let your interests guide you. Debating a topic close to your heart can make the experience more engaging and fulfilling.

4. Research Potential Topics

Before finalizing your committee choice, look into the potential topics that might be debated. Assess if they intrigue you and if you're willing to invest time researching and understanding them.

5. Size and Dynamics

Some delegates thrive in the bustling environment of large committees, while others prefer the intimacy of smaller groups where individual voices are more prominent. Consider what setting you're most comfortable in.

6. Consider the Chairs and Organizers

The chairpersons or directors of a committee can influence the debate's flow and dynamics. If you're familiar with past MUNs or the organizers, consider their reputation or style.

7. Future Ambitions

If you're considering a career in a particular field, such as health or finance, aligning your committee choice with that ambition can be advantageous. It offers a simulated experience of real-world issues you might encounter in your chosen profession.

Choosing the right MUN committee is a blend of self-awareness, interest, and strategy. It's not merely about debating but about immersing yourself in a transformative experience. Remember, every committee, irrespective of its size or theme, offers invaluable lessons in diplomacy, negotiation, and global affairs. So, make your choice wisely, and embark on a journey of learning, collaboration, and global camaraderie.

Fun Activity :)

"MUN Adventure Journal"

Objective:

Help young learners explore the world of MUN committees, finding out which topics and roles excite them most, all through a fun journaling adventure!

Materials Needed:

- A small notebook or journal.

- Printed pictures or stickers of world flags, gavels, globes, etc.

- Colored pencils or markers.

- Printed brief descriptions of each committee type and a few topic ideas.

Instructions for the Kid:

1. **My MUN Adventure Begins!**

   - On the first page of your journal, write "My MUN Adventure!" and decorate it with the pictures or stickers. This is the start of your exploration journey!

2. **Discovering Committees:**

   - On the next pages, you will paste or draw the different committees: General Assembly, WHO, Crisis Committee, and Historical Committee.

   - Under each committee title, stick or write the brief description you have. This will help you remember what each committee is all about!

3. **Imaginary Committee Time:**

   - For each committee, think of a pretend scenario or problem the world is facing. Draw it or write it down.

* For example, under WHO, you might think of a mystery illness that turns people's hair yellow! Or for the Crisis Committee, imagine there's a dragon that needs a new home because his old cave got flooded!

4. **Solo Debate:**

   - Now, pretend you're a delegate (a fancy word for someone who talks and decides things in these committees). Write down three ideas or solutions for each problem you imagined.

   * For the blue hair illness, maybe scientists could make a special shampoo? Or maybe everyone decides that blue hair is cool, and they have a big blue hair parade!

5. **Reflect on Your Adventure:**

   - Which committee did you have the most fun imagining? Which problem was the coolest to solve? Write down your thoughts.

   - On a scale from 1 to 5, rank each committee based on how much you liked it (5 being super awesome!).

6. **Decorate Your Journal:**

   - Use your colored pencils or markers to add doodles, designs, or anything you like to your journal pages.

7. **Conclusion:**

   - On the last page, write, "My MUN Adventure Ends Here... For Now!" and give yourself a big star or sticker for completing your journey.

Benefits:

The "MUN Adventure Journal" allows kids to explore the MUN landscape in a creative, independent manner. By imagining scenarios and solutions, they not only learn about the different committees but also practice problem-solving and critical thinking. Plus, the journal serves as a keepsake of their MUN adventure!

Chapter 7

KEY MUN TERMINOLOGY: SPEAKING THE DIPLOMATIC LANGUAGE

As you delve into the world of Model United Nations (MUN), you'll encounter a unique lexicon that underpins the intricate dance of diplomacy and debate. Understanding this terminology is crucial not only for effective participation but also to immerse oneself fully in the MUN experience. This chapter introduces you to some fundamental MUN terms, ensuring you can confidently navigate your way through any conference.

1. **Delegate:** A participant in an MUN conference representing a member state or non-governmental entity. Delegates debate, negotiate, and draft resolutions in their assigned committees.

2. **Resolution:** A formal document outlining proposed solutions to the issues being discussed. Resolutions are debated, amended, and then voted upon by the committee.

3. **Draft Resolution (DR):** A resolution before it's formally introduced to the committee. It's during this stage that delegates collaborate and seek co-sponsorship.

4. **Clause:** Individual components or sections of a resolution. Each clause addresses a specific aspect or proposed solution to the issue.

5. **Sponsors:** Delegates who have played a significant role in writing and advocating for a draft resolution.

6. **Co-sponsors:** Delegates who support a draft resolution and wish to be associated with it, although they might not have actively contributed to its writing.

7. **Point of Order:** A formal interjection by a delegate if they believe the committee's rules of procedure are being violated. It requires immediate attention and can't be used to comment on the topic being discussed.

8. **Point of Information:** A delegate's request to ask a question. Depending on the rules, it can be directed to the chair or another delegate.

9. **Point of Personal Privilege:** Used when a delegate has a personal concern or issue, such as not being able to hear another speaker.

10. **Moderated Caucus:** A flexible, fast-paced discussion format where delegates raise their placards to speak on the topic at hand. The chair controls the speaking order.

11. **Unmoderated Caucus:** A break from formal debate where delegates can freely move around and discuss, usually used for negotiations or drafting resolutions.

12. **Yield:** After a delegate gives a formal speech, they can yield their remaining time either to another delegate, to questions, or back to the chair.

13. **Roll Call:** At the beginning of a committee session, the chair calls out each member state's name to establish attendance.

14. **Quorum:** The minimum number of member states that must be present for the committee to officially conduct its business.

15. **Motion:** A proposal made by a delegate. For example, a delegate might motion to move into an unmoderated caucus or to introduce a draft resolution.

16. **Voting Bloc:** A group of delegates that form a temporary alliance based on shared interests or objectives.

This terminology, while seemingly complex, becomes second nature as you participate in MUN conferences. Remember, MUN is not just about mastering the jargon but understanding the essence behind each term. They represent the procedures and etiquettes of international diplomacy. As you familiarize yourself with these terms, you'll find yourself better equipped to engage in debates, form alliances, and work towards solutions that reflect the spirit of collaborative diplomacy that the United Nations embodies.

Fun Activity :)

"MUN Terminology Bingo"

Objective:

To familiarize young learners with the essential MUN terminology in an enjoyable and interactive manner.

Materials Needed:

- Pre-made Bingo cards with the MUN terms written in each square (mix up the order for each card).

- Small tokens or stickers to mark off called words.

- A bowl or hat with each term written on a separate slip of paper.

Instructions for the Kid:

1. **Setting up the Bingo Card:**

   - Place your Bingo card in front of you. Look at all the MUN terms written on it. Do any look familiar?

   - Read each word aloud, trying to remember what it might mean.

2. **Drawing the Terms:**

   - Each term will be drawn from the bowl one at a time. As the term is drawn, a brief, fun definition or example will be given for it.

   * For example, when "Delegate" is drawn, you could say, "This is someone just like you! They represent a country and talk about important stuff."

3. **Playing Bingo:**

   - As each term is drawn and defined, if you have that term on your card, place a token or sticker over it.

- The goal is to get five in a row horizontally, vertically, or diagonally. When you do, shout "Bingo!"

4. **Becoming a MUN Star:**

   - Once someone gets a Bingo, everyone can discuss the terms on the winning row. Try to explain what each term means in your own words or give a fun example. The more you talk about it, the better you'll understand!

5. **Bonus Round:**

   For those wanting an extra challenge, try the "MUN Story Challenge." Using the terms from your winning Bingo row, create a short story or scene. For example, if your row had "Delegate," "Resolution," and "Roll Call," maybe you can imagine a scenario where a delegate is late for roll call because they were busy writing a resolution about the importance of ice cream for all!

Benefits:

"MUN Terminology Bingo" provides a playful way for kids to engage with and learn MUN jargon. Not only does it foster retention through repetition in a game format, but the added discussion and story challenge ensure deeper comprehension and application of each term. By the end, young learners will feel more comfortable and excited about stepping into the world of MUN!

Chapter 8

DRAFTING A RESOLUTION: CRAFTING SOLUTIONS THROUGH DIPLOMACY

The crux of any Model United Nations (MUN) conference lies in the resolutions that are debated, amended, and eventually passed or failed. These resolutions are not just documents; they are the tangible output of hours of research, debate, negotiation, and collaboration. In this chapter, we will delve into the nuances of drafting a resolution, understanding its structure, and the art of collaborating with fellow delegates.

The Anatomy of a Resolution: Diving Deeper

In MUN, a resolution is the culmination of all the research, discussions, debates, and negotiations that delegates undergo. Like any formal document, resolutions follow a precise structure that ensures clarity, coherence, and diplomatic elegance. Let's delve deeper into the structure of a resolution and understand each section's significance and intricacies.

1. Header

The resolution's header provides a snapshot of the most basic yet essential information related to the resolution.

Committee Name: Indicates which UN body or committee is discussing the topic. This helps in understanding the jurisdiction and the scope of the resolution.

Topic: Clearly states the specific issue or problem being addressed, ensuring that readers instantly grasp the resolution's main subject.

Sponsors and Co-sponsors: Sponsors are the primary authors of the resolution, while co-sponsors are countries that support it. This distinction provides insights into the driving forces behind the resolution and its broader endorsement.

Preambulatory Clauses

These clauses lay the groundwork for the resolution. They set the stage and context. They're written in the present tense and give readers an understanding of the background and the urgency of the matter.

Referencing Past Actions: Often, these clauses refer to previous resolutions, conventions, or treaties related to the topic, emphasizing the continuity of international efforts.

Example: "Recalling Resolution 1234 on the protection of tropical rainforests,"

Expressing Emotions or Concerns: Some preambulatory clauses might express concerns, hopes, acknowledgments, or any other sentiments that reflect the international community's feelings about the issue.

Example: "Deeply disturbed by the unabated rise in global pollution levels,"

Providing Context: By citing data, trends, or specific events, these clauses can further shed light on the topic's gravity.

Example: "Noting with appreciation the efforts by NGOs in promoting sustainable agriculture,"

Operative Clauses

Operative clauses are the actionable part of the resolution. They provide clear directives or suggestions on how to address the issue.

Verb Choice: The verbs used in these clauses are definitive, indicating the level of commitment or action. For instance, "Decides" or "Demands" have a stronger tone than "Encourages" or "Suggests."

Specificity: These clauses should be specific, providing clear guidelines or steps to be taken. Vague or ambiguous clauses can dilute the resolution's impact.

Example: "2. Calls upon member states to increase their annual funding for renewable energy research by 10% for the next decade;"

4. Sub-clauses or Sub-sets:

These are essentially the 'details' that complement an operative clause. They provide depth, nuance, and specificity.

Detailing Mechanisms: If an operative clause calls for the creation of a new body or fund, the sub-clauses can detail its functions, members, funding sources, etc.

Example: "3. Proposes the establishment of an International Green Fund (IGF);

    a. Tasking the IGF with financing reforestation projects in regions with acute deforestation;

    b. Allocating an initial budget of $1 billion to the IGF sourced from contributions by member states;"

Elaborating on Steps: Sub-clauses can break down complex processes or suggestions into more digestible steps, ensuring clarity.

Example: "4. Recommends enhancing educational infrastructure in rural areas;

    a. By constructing at least two schools in every rural district by 2025;

    b. Ensuring internet connectivity in all such schools for online education and resources."

In essence, a resolution is more than a mere document; it's a testament to diplomatic collaboration. By understanding its structure and nuances, MUN delegates can craft impactful resolutions that not only address pressing global issues but also reflect the spirit of international cooperation.

The Dance of Diplomacy: Collaborating with Fellow Delegates

In the realm of Model United Nations (MUN), the essence of diplomacy isn't just about understanding global issues but about navigating the nuanced dynamics of interpersonal relations. Crafting a resolution, central to the MUN experience, is a harmonious blend of research, negotiation, and collaboration. The art of working with other delegates is pivotal in ensuring the resolution's success.

1. Identifying Potential Allies

The early stages of committee sessions often reveal delegates with whom your country shares common interests or policy stances.

Active Listening: Pay keen attention during the general speakers' list. Delegates often lay out their primary concerns and stances, providing clues about potential allies.

Engage in Side Discussions: During unmoderated caucuses or breaks, approach potential allies. Engage them in brief conversations, testing the waters for potential collaboration.

2. The Art of Co-Drafting

Once you've identified potential allies and formed a bloc, the intricate task of drafting begins.

Divide and Conquer: Given the comprehensive nature of resolutions, it's beneficial to divide topics or sections among the group based on expertise or interest.

Regular Check-ins: Ensure that the group meets periodically to review each section, ensuring consistency and coherence in the document.

3. Navigating Diplomatic Waters

Even among allies, differences of opinion are natural. Diplomacy lies in navigating these differences.

Constructive Debates: Encourage open discussions, allowing each delegate to express concerns or suggestions. Such debates often lead to a richer and more nuanced resolution.

Prioritize: Understand which points are non-negotiable and where compromises can be made without diluting the resolution's essence.

4. Broadening the Support Base

A resolution's strength is often gauged by the number of co-sponsors it garners.

Outreach: Once your bloc has a draft, approach other delegates. Highlight key points that might appeal to them, aiming to expand your list of co-sponsors.

Flexibility: Sometimes, to gain wider support, minor tweaks or additions to the resolution might be necessary. Be prepared for this, always weighing the broader objective against specific details.

5. Evolving and Adapting the Resolution

As the committee session progresses, feedback, debates, and fresh insights might necessitate changes to the resolution.

Active Engagement: During debates on your resolution, actively engage with critiques and suggestions. This helps in identifying areas of contention that might require amendments.

Collective Decision Making: When considering amendments, reconvene with your bloc. Discuss the merits of each amendment, ensuring that decisions made align with the group's broader vision.

Crafting a resolution in MUN mirrors real-world diplomacy, demanding research prowess, persuasive skills, and the ability to collaborate effectively. When delegates embrace these facets, they not only inch closer to a successful resolution but also experience the heart of MUN – mutual understanding, consensus-building, and global cooperation.

Fun Activity:)

"Resolution Builder"

Objective:

Allow young learners to dive into the world of resolutions, understanding its structure and nuances, and guiding them to craft their very own resolution on a topic of their interest.

Materials Needed:

- Notebook or writing pad.

- Pens, colored pencils, or markers.

- Sample 'starter' resolution (provided below).

Instructions:

1. **Introduction to the Starter Resolution:**

   You're provided with a simple 'starter' resolution on a fun topic, for instance, "Introducing a Pet Day at School."

   Sample Starter Resolution:

   Header:

   Committee: Student Council

   Topic: Introducing a Pet Day at School

   Sponsors: [Your Name Here]

   Preambulatory Clauses:

   - Recognizing the joy pets bring into our lives,

   - Noting the educational benefits of learning about different animals,

   Operative Clauses:

   1. Proposes the introduction of a Pet Day at school every year.

   2. Encourages students to bring in a variety of pets, ensuring safety and comfort for all animals.

2. **Choose Your Topic:**

   If you're happy with "Introducing a Pet Day at School," great! If not, think about another topic you're passionate about. Maybe "Having More Art Classes in School" or "Creating a School Garden."

3. **Become Your Own Committee:**

   Think about your role. Are you representing the student body, a specific class year, or maybe a club? Write down the committee's name.

4. **Dive into Preambulatory Clauses:**

   Based on your topic, list down reasons, emotions, or past actions/events related to it. Why is your topic important? What's the background?

5. **Craft Your Operative Clauses:**

   Now, it's action time! What do you propose should be done about your topic? Be specific and clear. Remember, these are the steps you suggest should be taken to address the topic.

6. **Review and Refine:**

   Read through your resolution. Make sure each point is clear and makes sense. Look for areas to add details or make the language more 'diplomatic.'

7. **Presentation:**

   Once you're happy with your resolution, give it a title page. Maybe even illustrate or decorate it. You've now created your very own MUN-style resolution!

8. **Reflect:**

   Think about the process. What did you learn about the topic you chose? How did you feel playing the role of a delegate, making decisions and crafting solutions?

Benefits:

"Resolution Builder" provides a deep dive into the MUN resolution crafting process in an individualized manner. This activity encourages independent research, critical thinking, and creative writing. By the end, kids will have a tangible document they crafted, showcasing their understanding of MUN and their passion for a topic of their choice.

MUN PROCEDURES AND RULES

The Model United Nations (MUN) simulates the procedures of the actual United Nations, and understanding these procedures is essential for effective participation. This chapter breaks down the fundamental MUN rules and procedures, from points and motions to the intricacies of voting.

Points and Motions

These are the basic tools at a delegate's disposal to navigate the flow of the committee session.

1. Points

Point of Personal Privilege: Relates to personal discomfort, such as not being able to hear a speaker.

Point of Order: Raised when a delegate believes there's a breach in the committee's rules.

Point of Information: Used to ask questions to another delegate after their speech.

Point of Inquiry: Used to ask questions to the Executive Board of your Committee regarding any procedure.

2. Motions

Motion to Move into a Moderated Caucus: Proposes a time-limited discussion where delegates raise their placards to speak.

Motion to Move into an Unmoderated Caucus: Proposes a free-form discussion period, allowing delegates to move around and discuss freely.

Motion to Close Debate: Seeks to end the discussion on a particular topic or resolution and move to voting.

Formal vs. Informal Sessions

Understanding the difference between these two types of sessions is key to strategizing your participation.

Formal Sessions: This is the default mode of the committee where delegates give speeches, make points, and raise motions. Decorum is strictly maintained, and delegates speak in third person.

Informal Sessions (or Unmoderated Caucus): A break from the formality where delegates can freely converse, negotiate, and draft resolutions. It's a chance to build alliances and strategize.

Voting Procedures

Voting is the culmination of debates and signifies the committee's collective decision on resolutions or other matters.

1. **Substantive Votes:** These votes pertain to the main content, such as voting on entire resolutions or amendments.

    Voting by Roll Call: A method where the Chair calls out each country's name, and they orally announce their vote.

Voting by Placard: Delegates raise their placards to indicate their vote.

2. **Procedural Votes:** Concerned with the functioning of the committee, such as motions to move into caucuses. No abstentions are allowed in procedural votes.

3. **Types of Votes**

   In Favor: Supporting the resolution or amendment.

   Against: Opposing the resolution or amendment.

   Abstain: Not casting a vote in favor or against. Usually signifies neutrality or indecision.

In essence, mastering MUN procedures and rules is like learning the rules of a strategic game. By understanding these intricacies, delegates can effectively steer the direction of debate, negotiate with clarity, and ensure their voice is heard in the committee. This chapter serves as a foundational guide, but always remember to review the specific rules of procedure for each individual MUN conference, as they might have variations or unique rules.

Fun Activity :)

"MUN Rules Mastery Challenge"

Objective:

Equip young learners with a practical understanding of the rules and procedures of Model United Nations (MUN) through hands-on activities and challenges.

Materials Needed:

- Notebook or writing pad.

- Pens or markers.

- A timer.

- Sample 'scenario cards' (provided below).

- Small flags or placards (can be made from cardboard or paper).

Instructions:

1. **Warm-Up: MUN Glossary Creation**

   Using your notebook, create a glossary of MUN terms you learned from Chapter 9. Include terms like "Point of Personal Privilege," "Moderated Caucus," "Substantive Votes," etc., and write a brief definition for each.

2. **Scenario Challenge:**

   You'll be presented with various MUN scenarios. Your task? Decide the appropriate point, motion, or action to take.

   Sample Scenarios:

   - You can't hear the delegate speaking.

   - You want to shift the committee to a structured discussion about deforestation.

   - You believe a delegate has spoken out of turn.

   Write down your responses for each scenario.

3. **Timer Test: Quick Points and Motions**

   Set a timer for 2 minutes. How quickly can you list down all the points and motions you remember? Try it out!

4. **Formal vs. Informal Session Role-play:**

   Imagine you're in a formal session discussing "Climate Change." Write down a short formal speech, addressing the committee. Remember, use the third person!

   Switch gears and imagine you're in an informal session with a fellow delegate. Draft a brief dialogue, discussing collaboration on a resolution about "Renewable Energy."

5. **Voting Practice:**

   Using the small flags or placards you've made:

   - Practice a "Voting by Placard" round. Propose a mock resolution (e.g., "More playground time during school hours") and vote: In Favor, Against, or Abstain.

   - Write down three countries (e.g., USA, Brazil, Japan). Practice a "Voting by Roll Call" round by announcing each country's name and orally casting their vote.

6. **Reflection Time:**

   Review the activities and challenges you've completed. Which rules or procedures do you feel most confident about? Which ones do you find tricky?

Benefits:

The "MUN Rules Mastery Challenge" allows young learners to internalize MUN procedures through interactive exercises. By engaging in these activities, they won't just read about the rules; they'll practice them, helping cement their understanding and preparing them for actual MUN participation.

Chapter 10

BEFORE YOU GO FOR MODEL UN CONFERENCES

The heart and soul of Model United Nations (MUN) lies in its conferences. These events, which can range from local gatherings to massive international conclaves, offer delegates the opportunity to put their knowledge and skills into practice, simulate real-world diplomacy, and forge lasting relationships. As you gear up for a Model UN conference, here's what you need to know.

Preparing for the Big Day

Success at an MUN conference often stems from thorough preparation.

1. **Research Your Country/Role:** Understand the history, culture, political stance, and foreign policy of the country you're representing. This will guide your approach and arguments.

2. **Understand the Topic:** Dive deep into the topic assigned to your committee. Understand its nuances, key stakeholders, and potential solutions.

3. **Practice Public Speaking:** Confidence in speech is vital. Practice speaking clearly, concisely, and persuasively.

4. **Draft Preliminary Documents:** Prepare a position paper or any required preliminary resolutions. Even if they're not mandatory, they'll aid in understanding and shaping your stance.

5. **Pack Essential:** Ensure you have notepads, pens, the conference schedule, any draft resolutions, and formal attire ready.

What to Expect

While every MUN conference has its unique flavor, there are some universal experiences you can anticipate.

1. **Opening Ceremony:** Most conferences start with a formal introduction, often featuring guest speakers.

2. **Committee Sessions:** The crux of the event. Engage in debates, negotiations, and drafting in your assigned committee.

3. **Crisis Scenarios (in certain committees):** Simulated real-time events that require quick thinking and collaborative problem-solving.

4. **Workshops & Seminars:** Some conferences offer sessions on topics like international relations, public speaking, or specific global challenges.

5. **Closing Ceremony:** A concluding event where resolutions are presented and awards (Best Delegate, Honorable Mention, etc.) are given out.

Making New Friends

MUN conferences aren't just about debates and resolutions; they're social hubs.

1. **Networking Opportunities:** Interact with students from various backgrounds, schools, or even countries. It's a chance to expand your network and learn from others.

2. **Collaborative Spirit:** While MUN is competitive, the essence lies in collaboration. Forge partnerships, strategize together, and work towards consensus.

3. **Social Events:** Many conferences have socials or cultural nights. Embrace these moments to relax, bond, and make lasting friendships.

4. **Staying Connected:** Collect contacts, and keep in touch post-conference. The relationships you cultivate at MUN can lead to future collaborations, both academically and professionally.

To sum up, Model UN conferences are transformative experiences that offer a blend of learning, debate, and camaraderie. As you step into this world of diplomacy simulation, go in with an open mind, a prepared stance, and a willingness to connect. The skills and relationships you garner from these events can leave a lasting impact on your academic and professional journey.

Chapter 11

HOW TO START OR JOIN AN MUN CLUB AT SCHOOL

Model United Nations (MUN) provides students an avenue to dive into the world of diplomacy, international relations, and negotiation. Establishing or joining an MUN club at school is an exciting step that opens up a realm of opportunities. Here's a step-by-step guide to help you through the process.

Finding an Advisor

Having a faculty advisor is pivotal in navigating the logistics and institutional guidelines.

1. **Identifying Potential Advisors:** Seek out teachers or staff members who have an interest in global affairs, debate, or student leadership activities.

2. **Pitch the Idea:** Approach potential advisors with a clear vision. Explain the benefits of MUN, not just for students but also for the broader school community.

3. **Establish Roles:** Once onboard, work collaboratively. While the advisor provides guidance, remember, it's a student-driven endeavor.

Organizing Meetings

Consistent meetings lay the foundation of a successful MUN club.

1. **Schedule Regular Sessions:** Choose a fixed day and time. Weekly meetings are standard, allowing ample time for practice and preparation.
2. **Set an Agenda:** Each meeting should have a purpose. Whether it's training on MUN procedures, discussing global issues, or practicing public speaking, stay focused.
3. **Promote Inclusivity:** Ensure all members feel valued. Rotate roles, encourage open discussions, and welcome feedback.

Hosting Mini-Conferences

Hosting mini-MUN conferences can be a fantastic way to practice and promote the club.

1. **Choose a Theme:** Pick a relevant topic or global issue to center your mini-conference around.
2. **Allocate Roles:** Apart from delegates, you'll need chairs, secretariats, and logistical support. Distribute responsibilities among club members.
3. **Publicize the Event:** Use school notice boards, newsletters, and social media to create buzz. Invite other schools if feasible.
4. **Logistics:** Organize materials, set up committee rooms, and arrange for refreshments.
5. **Feedback Loop:** After the event, gather feedback. What went well? What can be improved? Use this as a learning experience.

Seeking External Support

Starting or joining an MUN club is a commendable initiative, and external support can provide valuable guidance. If you wish to have an experienced MUN organizer assist or even organize an MUN in your school, consider reaching out to experts in the field.

I with my extensive MUN background, am available to guide, mentor, or help organize MUN events. My goal is to foster the growth of MUN culture in schools and share my knowledge with budding diplomats. If you need my assistance, feel free to reach out at anas.llm@ icloud.com

In conclusion, whether you're taking the first step to start an MUN club or looking to enhance an existing one, the journey is bound to be enriching. Embrace the challenges, celebrate the successes, and remember – it's all about learning, collaborating, and making a difference.

Chapter 12

PEACEFUL SETTLEMENT OF DISPUTES IN THE UN CONTEXT AND ITS RELEVANCE TO MUN

The United Nations, as a harbinger of international peace and security, places significant emphasis on the peaceful settlement of disputes. This is not only vital to prevent conflicts but also to maintain the credibility of the international system. For Model United Nations (MUN) participants, understanding these mechanisms is pivotal, as it forms the backbone of many committee discussions and resolutions.

Negotiation in the UN and Its Relevance to MUN

Negotiation, often hailed as the bedrock of diplomacy, is a quintessential tool for the peaceful settlement of disputes. At its essence, negotiation involves direct communication between conflicting parties with the intent to arrive at a mutual agreement. The United Nations, in its pursuit of global peace and diplomacy, actively champions this approach, emphasizing it before delving into more formalized resolution mechanisms.

This commitment to negotiation is enshrined in the UN Charter, specifically under Chapter VI, which outlines the methods for the peaceful resolution of conflicts. Moreover, a myriad of UN Resolutions, especially those stemming from the General Assembly, fervently advocate for the use of negotiations to defuse tensions and address ongoing disputes. For budding diplomats and participants in the Model United Nations, understanding the rich tapestry of negotiation within the UN framework is invaluable. A key tip for MUN delegates is to immerse themselves in prior negotiation attempts related to their designated topic. By doing so, they gain invaluable historical insights, which not only enhance their comprehension but also act as foundational pillars when crafting nuanced resolutions and debating strategies.

Mediation in the UN Framework and its Significance in MUN

Mediation, a pivotal mechanism in the realm of conflict resolution, often proves instrumental in carving out pathways to peace, especially when entrenched parties struggle to see eye to eye. At its core, mediation involves the intervention of a neutral third party, who facilitates dialogue between the disputing entities, steering them towards a consensus without dictating or imposing any specific resolution. The United Nations, recognizing the profound value of this approach, often deploys it to diffuse escalating tensions and nurture diplomatic dialogues. Integral to this effort are Special Envoys or Representatives appointed by the UN Secretary-General, who often don the hat of mediators in contentious situations. To bolster this endeavor, the UN has also institutionalized the Mediation Support Unit, which extends critical expertise, resources, and logistical backing to mediation missions globally.

For MUN enthusiasts, understanding the nuanced role of UN-mediated efforts is crucial. A strategic tip for delegates would be to delve deep into the methodologies and strategies adopted by iconic UN mediators in past conflicts. By assimilating these tactics and approaches, not only do they enrich their own diplomatic arsenal, but they also gain an edge in committee simulations, embodying the very essence of UN-backed mediation in action.

Conciliation in the UN Framework and its Role in MUN

Conciliation, though less invoked compared to its counterparts, holds a unique position in the spectrum of dispute resolution mechanisms. Rather than just facilitating dialogue or mediating between conflicting parties, conciliation delves into an investigative approach to discern the underlying factors of a dispute. Essentially, a neutral committee, or a conciliation commission, is tasked with dissecting the nature and nuances of the disagreement, post which they propose an informed and balanced solution for consideration. Within the expansive architecture of the United Nations, conciliation has found mention and endorsement in several resolutions, even if its deployment has been sporadic.

These conciliation commissions serve as instruments to navigate disputes that have proven resistant to traditional diplomatic overtures. For those diving into the world of Model United Nations, recognizing the potential of conciliation can be pivotal. As a delegate, when confronted with stalemates or impasses where conventional resolutions seem ineffective or redundant, championing the establishment of a conciliation committee can be a strategic masterstroke. It not only mirrors a deep understanding of international dispute resolution but also showcases a knack for innovative and informed diplomatic maneuvers.

Arbitration within the UN Ecosystem and its Significance in MUN

Arbitration, as a structured yet flexible form of dispute resolution, holds notable weight in international deliberations. Distinct from traditional courtroom setups, it offers an avenue where disputing entities can have their grievances addressed in a binding manner, yet outside the formal trappings of a court. The arbitrators, selected by mutual consent of the parties involved, thoroughly evaluate the contention and render a decision that is contractually binding.

In the grand scheme of the United Nations' conflict resolution toolkit, arbitration enjoys significant recognition, particularly in commercial and trade spheres. A paramount example of this is the United Nations Commission on International Trade Law (UNCITRAL). Established to promote the progressive harmonization and unification of international trade law, UNCITRAL has proffered a set of rules tailored for arbitration procedures, thereby guiding and standardizing this form of dispute settlement in global trade contexts.

Model United Nations participants, equipped with the knowledge of arbitration and its nuances, can harness its potential in committee debates and negotiations. Especially in scenarios involving contentious issues between nations hesitant about appealing to formal courts like the International Court of Justice (ICJ), proposing arbitration emerges as a savvy diplomatic move. It suggests a compromise – a method that offers the legitimacy and binding nature of a court decision without resorting to the formal international judiciary. For delegates, mastering the dynamics of arbitration can elevate their position, demonstrating a holistic understanding of global dispute mechanisms and the ability to navigate and employ them adeptly.

Judicial Settlement: The Pinnacle of International Dispute Resolution and its Role in MUN

An epitome of global legal recourse, the judicial settlement stands as the ultimate mechanism for addressing disputes between nations. This process, undertaken before a revered international tribunal, imparts both gravitas and finality to the decisions made therein.

The International Court of Justice (ICJ), an illustrious arm of the United Nations, exemplifies this mechanism. Heralded by the UN

Charter, the ICJ possesses the authority and mandate to adjudicate disputes between member states. Functioning as the principal judicial body of the UN, its judgments carry not just a binding effect on the parties involved but also often pave the way for the evolution of international law. Each decision, meticulously reasoned and detailed, contributes a chapter to the ever-growing annals of global jurisprudence.

For those embarking on the Model United Nations journey, the realm of judicial settlements, and more specifically the ICJ, presents a unique arena of engagement. Especially when simulating the ICJ committee, a comprehensive grasp of the court's past landmark cases becomes indispensable. These judgments, laden with legal principles and interpretations, serve as touchstones – guiding delegates in forming their contentions, shaping their strategies, and constructing persuasive arguments. In this committee, more than any other, the law's letter and spirit intertwine, and delegates must deftly navigate both. By delving into the ICJ's rich legacy, MUN participants can not only bolster their legal acumen but also experience the profound impact of legal mechanisms in shaping international relations.

The peaceful settlement of disputes is integral to the functioning of the UN. MUN participants, by deeply understanding and embodying these mechanisms, not only enrich their MUN experience but also imbibe the principles on which the real-world United Nations operates. This knowledge bridges the gap between simulation and reality, and fosters a generation that truly believes in diplomacy and dialogue.

Chapter 13

REGIONAL ORGANIZATIONS - SPECIALIZED AGENCIES AND INTERNATIONAL NON-GOVERNMENT AGENCIES IN MUN

Introduction

In the vast realm of international relations, various organizations play pivotal roles in shaping global policy, addressing regional concerns, and fostering cooperation. Among them, regional organizations, specialized agencies, and international non-governmental agencies stand out as dynamic entities, each contributing uniquely to the global landscape. For MUN enthusiasts, understanding these organizations can enhance the depth of debate, offer diverse solutions, and elevate the overall quality of simulations.

Regional Organizations in the MUN Context

In the intricate web of international relations, regional organizations stand as shining beacons of collective regional aspiration and action.

These entities, deeply entrenched in the geography, history, or shared cultural ties of their member states, serve as pivotal platforms to address issues that resonate within specific parts of the globe. For instance, the African Union (AU), with its focus on the unique challenges faced by the African continent, champions causes like regional security and socio-economic development. On the other hand, the Association of Southeast Asian Nations (ASEAN) exemplifies a congregation of nations that, despite their diverse cultures and histories, come together with a unified vision of cooperation and mutual growth for Southeast Asia. For Model United Nations participants, especially those representing a member of such regional organizations, understanding this collaborative dynamic is imperative. In debates, these delegates should emphasize collective stances shaped by their regional bodies, making reference to past resolutions and agreements within these organizations. By doing so, they can advocate for solutions that not only resonate on a global scale but also cater to the regional intricacies and shared aspirations of their represented blocs.

Specialized Agencies in the MUN Landscape

As we navigate the sprawling ecosystem of international relations and global governance, specialized agencies emerge as critical pillars. While they operate autonomously, these organizations closely collaborate with the United Nations, each honing in on its niche area of expertise to address global challenges in a comprehensive manner. For instance, the World Health Organization (WHO), stands at the forefront of the global health arena, developing policies, conducting research, and coordinating responses to health emergencies. Similarly, the International Monetary Fund (IMF) plays a pivotal role in the realm of international finance, promoting monetary cooperation, ensuring financial stability, and offering economic advice to its member countries. For Model United Nations enthusiasts, understanding the depth and breadth of these specialized agencies is crucial. During debates, especially when topics touch upon areas like health or economics, it's a game-changer to reference the reports, guidelines, and advisories of these expert bodies. Integrating findings and recommendations from these agencies into one's arguments not only demonstrates thorough research but also lends unparalleled credibility, making a delegate's case more compelling in the simulated UN environment.

International Non-Governmental Agencies: Catalysts of Global Change

Within the vast mosaic of international entities, International Non-Governmental Organizations (INGOs), commonly termed NGOs in MUN committees, occupy a distinctive and pivotal space. Operating outside the framework of state governance, INGOs exemplify the profound impact that non-state actors can exert on the global stage. Their roles span a broad spectrum – from direct humanitarian intervention and grassroots advocacy to influencing international policy-making with their expert insights.

Take for instance Doctors Without Borders (Médecins Sans Frontières). This esteemed medical organization transcends borders and political affiliations to deliver urgent medical care in conflict zones, disaster-stricken areas, and regions facing epidemics. Their interventions are a testament to the profound impact of humanitarian action in the face of adversity. On the other hand, Amnesty International stands as a beacon for human rights. By documenting human rights abuses and mobilizing public opinion, they apply pressure on governments and institutions to respect and enforce international human rights laws and standards.

For Model United Nations participants, integrating the work and findings of INGOs into their strategy is paramount. These organizations often possess ground-level data and first-hand testimonies, offering a lens into the realities often detached from diplomatic parlance. By citing INGO reports and testimonies, delegates can not only substantiate their arguments but also humanize them, presenting a holistic picture that encompasses both the macro and micro dimensions of an issue. In the theater of MUN, where evidence-based arguments reign supreme, the voice and validation of INGOs can significantly bolster a delegate's stance.

While the United Nations remains a focal point in MUN debates, these diverse organizations enrich discussions, offering varied perspectives and multifaceted solutions. By understanding and integrating these entities into their arguments and resolutions, MUN participants can craft more realistic, well-rounded, and impactful positions.

Chapter 14

POWER, AUTHORITY, AND LEGITIMACY: THE FOUNDATIONS OF POLITICAL STRUCTURES

In the realms of political science and international relations, the triad of power, authority, and legitimacy stands central. These intertwined concepts help in understanding the dynamics of governance, international diplomacy, and the very essence of political interaction among and within states. For an MUN delegate, grasping these principles is fundamental to navigating the complex terrains of global politics.

1. Power: The Ability to Influence

Power, in the intricate web of international relations, is an entity's quintessential ability to sway or influence another. This might manifest overtly or subtly, directly impacting decisions or shaping perceptions indirectly. One can envisage power as a spectrum. On one end, there's "hard power," characterized by tangible assets: a nation's military arsenal that can be paraded in a show of might or its economic clout evident in trade negotiations. This is the overt, measurable strength that can coerce, incentivize, or deter. However, on the other end of this spectrum lies the more nuanced "soft power." It's intangible, yet just as compelling. Soft power weaves its influence through cultural exports, from the allure of Hollywood to the global resonance of K-pop. It's the finesse of diplomacy, where words craft narratives and mold alliances. For MUN participants, understanding this duality is pivotal. When stepping into the shoes of a nation's representative, one must ask: Where does the nation's strength lie? Is it wielding economic sanctions as tools of persuasion, or is it captivating hearts through cultural diplomacy, positioning itself as a global ambassador?

2. Authority: The Right to Exercise Power

Authority is the prism through which power is not just wielded but also legitimized. It is the sanctified right to exercise influence, grounding the use of power within a framework of acceptance and legitimacy. Think of it as the difference between influence driven by might versus the one driven by right. Consider the contrasting images of a mob boss who, while undeniably powerful within his domain, rules through sheer intimidation, and a police officer, whose directive emanates from the very fabric of established law. The former showcases power in its raw form, unchecked by any recognized mandate, while the latter is an embodiment of authority.

Different societies and systems recognize various wellsprings of authority. Traditional authority takes its roots in age-old customs, practices, and often hereditary rights – the reverence for a tribal elder or a monarch, for instance. Charismatic authority, on the other hand, revolves around the magnetic allure of an individual. It's the draw of a leader's personal charm, which followers find irresistible. Then there's legal-rational authority, the backbone of modern governance structures. It's derived from codified laws, procedures, and institutions, lending a systematic legitimacy to power.

For those navigating the Model UN landscape, a nuanced grasp of authority is essential. Representing a nation or a leader isn't just about understanding their power but also recognizing the source of their authority. Is the monarch you represent revered because of age-old customs? Or is the president anchored in a framework of legal-rational authority, fortified by democratic mandates? Understanding these nuances can offer valuable insights into a delegate's approach and strategies.

3. Legitimacy: The Accepted Authority

Legitimacy stands as the foundation upon which authority firmly rests. It is the intangible thread weaving through the tapestry of governance, rendering authority not just recognized, but also respected. While authority denotes the right to exercise power, legitimacy is the beacon that ensures such power is broadly accepted, ensuring smooth governance. An entity might have the authority to lead or make decisions, but without the veneer of legitimacy, it risks constant challenges and potential upheaval.

Several elements shape legitimacy. The consent of the governed, for instance, is pivotal. When a population willingly recognizes and approves an authority, its decisions and directives are more likely to be accepted without resistance. Then there's the weight of historical right – claims that find their roots in age-old traditions, ancestral mandates, or historical milestones. Lastly, a more pragmatic dimension: performance. When an authority consistently meets the needs of its populace, ensuring prosperity, safety, and justice, it reinforces its own legitimacy.

For MUN participants, understanding legitimacy is as vital as grasping the tenets of power and authority. As a delegate, when representing a nation or organization, it's imperative to discern the legitimacy layers of its governance. Is the leadership accepted because of a democratic mandate, or is it due to historical reverence? Or perhaps, is there a lurking legitimacy crisis, with dissent and opposition bubbling under the surface? Such insights can steer your strategies, molding your approaches in discussions, negotiations, and resolutions.

In the intricate world of international relations, understanding the nuances of power, authority, and legitimacy is crucial. These concepts underpin the very fabric of diplomacy, negotiations, and global politics. As MUN delegates strive to emulate real-world diplomacy, a grasp of these foundational principles ensures a more realistic, informed, and impactful participation.

STEPPING FORWARD AS TOMORROW'S LEADERS

Dear Aspiring Delegates,

As we turn the page on this journey through the intricacies of Model United Nations, remember this isn't the end. Rather, it is the dawn of your voyage into a realm of leadership, diplomacy, and global understanding. Through these chapters, you've not only equipped yourself with knowledge but also taken the first steps toward molding your future self.

Leadership is not defined by the titles we hold but by the choices we make. The arena of MUN teaches us not merely the art of negotiation, but the essence of true leadership – one that believes in justice, equality, and the betterment of humanity. You're not just a participant in a simulation; you're a beacon of hope for the world that you'll soon inherit. You carry the torch of responsibility, to transform dialogue into action and dreams into reality.

Remember, the loudest voice is not always the most influential, but a voice that speaks for justice, truth, and righteousness always echoes across horizons. Do not shy away from challenges; instead, embrace them as stepping stones to your aspirations. In the face of injustice, never bow down. Instead, rise, speak, and act. History has shown us time and again that silence can be the greatest oppressor. Make your voice heard, no matter how tremulous it may initially sound. Over time, with conviction and courage, it will resonate.

The world outside may at times seem daunting, filled with complex challenges and nuanced issues. But remember, it's your world. Your feelings, beliefs, and ideas have every right to be expressed and considered. Do not be confined by the borders of hesitation or self-doubt. Leap forth with your beliefs and ideas, for they are the seeds of transformation.

As you venture forth, bear in mind that MUN isn't just about winning awards or mastering procedure. It's about nurturing empathy, understanding different perspectives, and coming together to find solutions for a united global community.

Become the leaders you were meant to be. Illuminate paths, bridge divides, and build a world where every voice matters, and every dream is cherished. We believe in you, and now, it's your turn to believe in yourself.

With hope for a brighter tomorrow and immense faith in your capabilities,

Anas Dhorajiwala.

P.S. For those who wish to further their journey, to share ideas, or seek guidance, I am always here to help. Together, we can create MUN conferences, foster dialogue, and mentor future leaders. You can always reach out to me at anas.llm@icloud.com. Let's shape the future, together.